T3-BQQ-989

THE CLAM THEATER

The Wesleyan Poetry Program: Volume 64

THE CLAM THEATER

by RUSSELL EDSON

WESLEYAN UNIVERSITY PRESS
Middletown, Connecticut

PS
3509
D583
C5

Copyright © 1966, 1968, 1969, 1971, 1972, 1973 by Russell Edson

Acknowledgement is gratefully made to the following periodicals, in the pages of which some of the poems in this book were first published: *The Beloit Poetry Journal; Caterpillar; Chelsea; Chicago Review; Crazy Horse; Doones; The Dragonfly; Hearse; kayak; Lillabullero; Pebble;* and *The Seneca Review.*

Library of Congress Cataloging in Publication Data
Edson, Russell.
    The clam theater.

    (The Wesleyan poetry program: v. 64)
    I. Title.
PS3509.D583C5   811'.5'2   72–11052
ISBN 0–8195–2064–0
ISBN 0–8195–1064–5 (pbk)

62297

Manufactured in the United States of America
First edition

For Frances

CONTENTS

THE CLAM THEATER

THE AGENT

. . . Assigned to you when your flesh was separating from your mother's, this shadow, who seeing the opportunity at hand, joined your presence, in such a way as some say the soul is given.

You have always caricatured me in my travels. I have seen you on mountains, and in dim cafes. I have seen you hold your head, your elbows on your knees; and while I was sad you were serene!

I seek a mastery over fate, of which you are, in objective witness, the agent of . . . I run away one night as you sleep, the trusting wife, whose borders have opened in the universal dark.

She feels in the morning among the sheets for the easy habit of her husband's shape — Now arc the earth, sweet dark, the law of umbra give you panic to search me out with your cunning speed of light!

THE ANCESTRAL MOUSETRAP

We are left a mousetrap, baited with cheese. We must not jar it, or our ancestor's gesture and pressure are lost, as the trap springs shut.

He has relinquished his hands to what the earth makes of flesh. Still, here in this mousetrap is caught the thumb print of his pressure.

A mouse would steal this with its death, this still unspent jewel of intent.

In a jewel box it is kept, to keep it from the robber-mouse; even as memory in the skull was kept, to keep it from the robber-worm, who even now is climbing a thief in the window of his eyes.

THE ANT FARM

In spite even of Columbus the world collapses and goes flat again.

The sky is a bell jar where a child in another scale watches his ant farm.

When the bored child yawns two thousand years pass.

Someday we have crashed to the playroom floor; the careless child knocks us over with his fire truck. . . . All that dirt lying in its broken sky.

Swept up, it is thrown into a garbage can at the back of the universe.

APE AND COFFEE

Some coffee had gotten on a man's ape. The man said, animal, did you get on my coffee?

No no, whistled the ape, the coffee got on me.

You're sure you didn't spill on my coffee? said the man.

Do I look like a liquid? peeped the ape.

Well you sure don't look human, said the man.

But that doesn't make me a fluid, twittered the ape.

Well I don't know what the hell you are, so just stop it, cried the man.

I was just sitting here reading the newspaper when you splashed coffee all over me, piped the ape.

I don't care if you are a liquid, you just better stop splashing on things, cried the man.

Do I look fluid to you? Take a good look, hooted the ape.

If you don't stop I'll put you in a cup, screamed the man.

I'm not a fluid, screeched the ape.

Stop it, stop it, screamed the man, you are frightening me.

THE ATTRACTIVE NUISANCE

At night a cloud threatens his window. It gets caught between that tree and his bedroom window.

It happens at night, just when he thinks he hears his social position slipping.

Actually, it's only a cloud wedging itself between his bedroom window and that tree which, had it been cut down years ago, would not now be creating an attractive nuisance, where stray clouds entrap themselves each night, threatening his window, and upstaging the real sounds of his social position, as it slips away through the night.

A weeping woman heard a slight roar.

Her tears had loosened the flesh of her cheeks and caused a small avalanche.

My goodness, she said as her left nostril fell out of her head.

But this only caused her to weep beyond even the first cause of her weeping.

My goodness, she said, now that I have something to really weep about it's ruining my face, and the more it ruins my face the more I have something to weep about.

My goodness, I must stop this weeping, even my lachrymal glands have fallen.

Soon her whole face fell. The plop of it startled her.

My goodness, she said.

THE BALDHEADED MAN / for C.

It is as if the oils or nutriments irrigating the garden of the head were to flow at last to the more comfortable south of the head.

Then, whatever is left of the ornament, that southern horseshoe of hair, he shaves, opening his entire scalp into a desert.

Perhaps he thinks he hates this head for losing its hair. But he thinks this in the very head he thinks he hates.

If you want to be bald, then be bald! he thinks as he punishes and vitalizes his head by shaving it.

He is making his head into a glans penis; disguising his balding with baldness.

A microscopic paleontologist coming to this desert will understand that even here was once a jungle thick with hair, wherein even the dandruff bird was wont to perch in the branches of its dark. . . .

THE BIRTH OF A SEEMINGLY
CLEVER IDEA

We are going by way of a cliff, the one overlooking the universe, where we lose the sea to the sky, the line of liquid and gas merging. . . . This strange earthly sill in the cosmic doorway.

With wings of bedsheets and animal bones we take a running leap over the cliff . . . and are found below tangled in bedsheets and animal bones.

We cannot get through the doorway. We can only die in our rubbish . . . a bravery which the universe ignores.

THE BLANK BOOK

The book was blank, all the words had fallen out.

Her husband said, the book is blank.

His wife said, a funny thing happened to me on my way to the present moment. I was shaking the book, to get all the typos out, and all of a sudden all the words and punctuation fell out too. Maybe the whole book was a typo?

And what did you do with the words? said her husband.

I made a package and mailed it to a fictitious address, she said.

But no one lives there. Don't you know, hardly anyone lives at fictitious addresses. There's barely enough reality there to provide even a mailing address, he said.

That's why I sent them there. Words all mixed up can suddenly coalesce into rumors and malicious gossip, she said.

But don't these blank pages also present a dangerous invitation to rumors and malicious gossip? Who knows what anyone might write in his absent-mindedness? Who knows what chance might do with such a dangerous invitation? he said.

Perhaps we shall have to send ourselves away to some fictitious address, she said.

Is it because words keep falling out of our mouths, words that could easily start rumors and malicious gossip? he said.

It is because, somehow, we keep falling out of ourselves, like detached shadows; shaking as if we could get all the typos out of our lives, she said.

Well, at least, if this doesn't hurt reality, it does, in fact, give reality a well earned rest.

18

A BOX OF WOMAN

A man buys a box of woman and blurrs into several men, vibrating as they tear to open their box of woman.

Out comes the heart, an alligator pear. The womb's an enema bag. And the cunt's an old wash rag. This leg's a hoe, the other a rake. . . . One tit's a cup of custard, the other a breast of roasted chicken. . . .

When taking a woman one should check the ingredients printed on the box. Look for more flesh than bone, more happiness than not. . . . More desire than aspirin.

THE BREAKFAST
THAT CAME TO DINNER

A sailor who was actually a bathtub merchant; or should I say a baker who was actually a fur trapper. . . . No no, I shall say a lunch that was actually a delayed breakfast, came to our house for dinner.

It was explained that while making its way in the streets it suddenly became confused and knocked on the first door, the one seen most prominently, though vaguely, at the height of its confusion.

We quite understand. No need to explain. Just in time for dinner. Here, let us hang up your pea jacket. We'll just put those bathtubs in our bathroom, they won't seem so out of place there. Your muffin hat, here, we'll put it on this hook. The animal skins and traps, we'll hang them in the hall closet.

Did you say you were lunch? Oh, I see, a delayed breakfast, sort of a brunch. Well, what's the difference, it's already suppertime. If we're not careful it'll be getting on to midnight snack time. Time is always running out. Then it becomes breakfast time again; then brunch, and so on. No wonder you were so confused.

You must get away someday early in the morning before the traffic, as it were, before the hunger, before we rise from our murdered sleep. . . .

Find yourself a nice kitchen table in a good normal home. Arrive just at breakfast time. The birds full at song. Lay out your pretty things, your dowry of bathtubs and traps — Yes, lay out your pretty things, your grapefruit juice and toast; pretend you are a bride — Pretend the kitchen is the bed of consummation.

THE BROKEN DAUGHTER

His daughter had broken. He took her to be repaired. . . . If you'll just pump-up her backside, and rewire her hair. . . .

This girl needs a whole new set of valves, and look at all those collision marks around her face, said the mechanic.

I just want her fixed-up enough to use around the house; for longer trips I have my wife.

THE BURNT POTATOES

In the mountains where anything you say becomes an echo, one hardly speaks lest all his secrets become mountain gossip.

What one says never has done, and one dares not put the complaint, Alfred, the potatoes are burnt.

Even across the valley, in those mountains that reflect these in their blue repose, where one in extremity goes seeking respite from burnt potatoes, one is likely to meet one's own words in echo, a slight bit winded by now, *Alfred, the potatoes are burnt!*

And so I whisper to Alfred, please don't burn the potatoes anymore, the mountains are alive with my complaints.

. . . Yet, should he not burn potatoes did he not come to greater fault? — Better always to burn potatoes if in this fault there is barrier to even greater fault. . . .

Still, if one cannot turn one's thoughts to words because of these parrot mountains, whose repertoire is built of perfect memory, thinking without release, the thought driven against its tongue, ricocheting back and forth in silent echo, until one has come nearly deaf with it!

The cure of course, is to open the windows, and to scream into the valley ALFRED, PLEASE DON'T BURN THE POTATOES! The whole world screaming back ALFRED, PLEASE DON'T BURN THE POTATOES!

Alfred holding his ears screams I PROMISE NOT TO BURN THE POTATOES AGAIN! And the whole world is screaming I PROMISE NOT TO BURN THE POTATOES AGAIN!

THE CASE

Your case . . . ?

Mine, which is the only excuse I give for opening it.

You are opening it.

Yes, it is opened by me, which is the only excuse I give for opening it.

And it has things inside of it. . . .

Yes, things are inside because I have put them there, each in its own recess.

Instruments?

Yes, an old shoe which people will say is simply an old shoe. It is in my case to associate its presence with this gingerbread man. . . . Then too, this rock, which is also to be noticed. . . . And this toy sailboat. . . .

These are things in your case.

These are things in my case. When I close my case they are still there. When I open my case I can see that. Because they are there they have probably been there all the time the case was closed. . . . I guess at this. I am confident that I shall not reverse my opinion. I am very well satisfied that what I have believed is so. I have made no contingency plans.

Then you are sure?

I am filled with confidence. I am closing my case because I have finished having it open. I am relatching its latch because I have concluded its excuse for being open by closing it.

Then it's closed . . . ?

Yes, because I have done that to it.

THE CELEBRITY / for J. B.

Did they look at me? They did. I hid. Did I hide? That would have been beneath me. No, rather I refused to be where others were looking. Can this be called hiding? Certainly not.

It is always possible to find a place somewhat less obvious than someplace else. People seem always to seek the light. One has only to avoid where the golden shaft of the setting sun streams through the window. Or is it the electric light, thoughtlessly left on, that silhouettes me in the bathroom doorway?

Is it planned that small theaters of light shall promote me to the view of others? Am I at core a celebrity? One of those persons destined for public life?

Certainly if people leave lights on, or the sun continues to shine, I shall be left no choice but to open my pants. Is that not what they seek of the celebrity? Surely this intimacy is the final flower of their craving.

I blush to think that this has always been the reason for the sun's rising each morning.

Very well, the gates have opened, and having once tasted the public attention, I am ready for the final devotion. Taking all leave of privacy then, I stepped into a public thoroughfare, the entire ornament of the flesh, hair and blob, paunch and wrinkle, displayed in complete and bewildering essence. Demonstrating my rump I blew farts in several frequencies. . . . Disappointed only that in my shyness I could not find the scum of ecstasy. . . .

24

A man had a son who was an anvil. And then sometimes he was an automobile tire.

I do wish you would sit still, said the father.

Sometimes his son was a rock.

I realize that you have quite lost boundary, where no excess seems excessive, nor to where poverty roots hunger to need. But should you allow time to embrace you to its bosom of dust, that velvet sleep, then were you served even beyond your need; and desire in sate was properly spilling from its borders, said the father.

Then his son became the corner of a room.

Don't don't, cried the father.

And then his son became a floorboard.

Don't don't, the moon falls there and curdles your wits into the grain of the wood, cried the father.

What shall I do? screamed his son.

Sit until time embraces you into the bosom of its velvet quiet, cried the father.

Like this? cried his son as his son became dust.

Ah, that is more pleasant, and speaks well of him, who having required much in his neglect of proper choice, turns now, on good advice, to a more advantageous social stance, said the father.

But then his son became his father.

Behold, the son is become as one of us, said the father.

His son said, behold, the son is become as one of us.

Will you stop repeating me, screamed the father.

Will you stop repeating me, screamed his son.

Oh well, I suppose imitation is the sincerest form of flattery, sighed the father.

Oh well, I suppose imitation is the sincerest form of flattery, sighed his son.

When they ask you your name your head knows what to say, it has the brain and the mouth. The rest is all a mobile pedestal.

But when the head replies it is talking only for itself. The mute feet have certain ideas. The left one might want to be called Speedy; perhaps the right one, High Stepper.

But the head says, Henry.

That physical presence that we take to be ourselves is like an endless childhood of sybling rivalry.

The right-hand, if you are right-handed, proves early to be the brighter one; the left-hand the less bright, the weaker twin.

And while the right-hand will learn to write with much facility, it never learns to speak.

The head is always quick to say, I am Henry.

The rest of the body, the mute feet, Speedy and High Stepper; the good hands, Squeezer and Pinch; the sleepy penis, who chooses to be Earnest, and who is downgraded and hidden from public view, until the proper moment when he rises, particularly in milady's estimate. . . . All know that for all of Henry's eloquence, he is but a field of hair; a rat with its tail down the body's back.

CINDERELLA'S LIFE AT THE CASTLE

After Cinderella married the prince she turned her attention to minutiae, using her glass slipper as a magnifying lens.

When at court she would wear orange peels and fish tins, and other decorous rubbish as found in back of the castle.

You are making me very nervous, said the prince.

But Cinderella continued to look at something through her glass slipper.

Did you hear me? said the prince.

Cinderella's mouth hung open as she continued to look at something through her glass slipper.

Did you hear me, did you hear me, did you hear me? screamed the prince.

They had started a hat factory . . . Basically in a dream . . . Entirely so when you think that the very foundation begins somewhere in the brain, when the brain is unlaced like a shoe, and like a shoe free of the conscious foot with its corns and calls.

An old brick factory full of men mad for making hats rises in the head like Atlantis once more above the waters. . . . It is remarkable how like a foot the head really is; I mean the toes, perhaps ornaments of hair; the hollow of the arch must certainly find its mouth, the heel is already a jaw. . . .

This is my theater. I sit in my head asleep. Theater in a clam. . . .

Amidst the wet flesh of the head madmen build hats; perhaps to lay cover over the broken mind; or to say the head is gone, and all it is is hat. . . . Only hats hung on the hooks of our necks. . . .

COLIC

The baby does not keep its brain; we keep finding it on the floor by its crib.

Grandmother is asked if a jackknife might be drawn through her hair; for it is known that the aged carry luck in the ancient silver of their curls.

Grandmother says, yes, but take care, for not only is luck stored there, but also the ornament that vanity celebrates.

Yes yes, Grandma, we would only burnish the instrument, to whet its appetite for luck, while vanity sleeps in the dreams of praises passed.

And so the instrument is readied in Grandma's luck, losing her only a few of the silver curls; gladly given, so we hope, to cure the baby's colic.

We pry open one of the fontanels with father's jackknife, pressing the baby's brain into its head, hoping that it takes root, or however else in secures itself under the bone; and, perhaps in that solitary confinement, that darkness, find those few attitudes properly appraising this world.

But even so, the baby throws up its brain again. And we conclude old hair carries no special luck, only the flowers of a vanity, worked slowly over the years into ornaments of silver.

Father says, let us pray.

29

THE CRADLE / for Jonathan

Because it made my grandmother seem older I was not allowed to become any older myself; and spent my life in a large cradle, big enough for a man, shaking my rattle and teething ring for grandma's smile.

One day after practicing for years I said, please let me grow up, grandma dearest.
Do you want to kill me, wretch, with your self-indulgence?
And so I waved my teething ring at her, and she smiled.

Sadly enough this did not save her life.
I have remained in this large cradle, big enough for a man, waiting for grandma to smile at me again.
I shake my rattle at night, it sounds like the fire of distant stars.

THE CRUCIFIXION

The car won't start. He wonders if he shouldn't just simply allow it not to.
Perhaps this would be better than lifting the hood and finding an ape bolted to the motor mounts, with a set of sparkplugs in its mouth instead of teeth.
But, even so, perhaps it is not a real ape. Perhaps it is just an ape-costume someone has thrown over the engine—Not a real ape crucified on the motor mounts, with bolts through its wrists and ankles.
Perhaps, even, it is just a bearskin rug fixed up to look like an ape. . . .
Yes, he decides he will simply allow his car not to start.

30

CURING GRANDMA'S DIZZINESS

Grandpa had invented how to make artificial grandpas.

Grandma said, it is too artificial.

But look how one surrogate boils his artificial artificial teeth in lye; another cuts his artificial corns; while still another prunes the artificial hair in his artificial nose. . . . Artificial agents representing me in every corner of the house, through all the chores of idleness and pleasure, said grandpa.

Stop it, stop it, it is too artificial, and it makes me dizzy, cried grandma — While you sit in the living room you are in the kitchen stealing cookies, and yet, all the while you are down in the cellar secretly and artificially drinking.

But grandma, why don't I make an artificial grandma; using the basic grandpa, with a few artificial changes, like the genitalia and the costuming. Then you can let the artificial grandma get artificially dizzy while watching all the artificial grandpas rushing against the artificial equilibrium of the artificial grandma, swaying in her artificial witness as she enters her artificial dizziness, said grandpa.

A DEATH

Even if newspapers are the washclothes of the world, we read them for signs, as the hunter reads dung.

So he taught his car a few tricks, like playing dead, or how to sit up and beg a cup of gasoline.

He pretends not to think too much of his remarkable machine, and reads a newspaper as if nothing were more important than a moment of murder, or a simple reversal of current trends.

Roll over, roll over. And his car rolls over and crushes him. (Naturally the car will have to be destroyed.) But he's in luck because the paper boy is just arriving to wipe him up with his evening paper.

A man placed a young tree in a coffin. It got sick and died.

Too bad, said his mother.

Yes, I was watching it; thinking, merely a passing nausea, a simple vomit and the system comes right again.

Too bad, said his mother.

But now I could see that it was really sick. So I ran down to the coffin-maker and said, there's something got itself awfully sick. He said it was my head. I said no, my head's fine, thank you; but I do need a coffin in an awful hurry.

When father got home father said, you did right in principle, but wrong in practice. Not that your intentions were wrong; but the act is of questionable taste. Not, of course, that you did not mean well. . . . However, you have given us an unfortunate circumstance — First, my dearest of sons, one must not bury something made of wood in another thing made of wood. This is burying the dead in the dead, so to speak, and might, if not looked after, cause a very serious infection; if not here, certainly in heaven.

Secondly, most dear of all my sons, you have run up a bill at the coffin-maker's, paid only from the monies set by for the time when I shall seek the privacy now being enjoyed by the young tree — You have disrobed your father and clothed the stranger. Not that I do not applaud the act that clothes the naked (there is even certain sexual modesty to it), and bespeaks the kind heart that bears not easily the need of another. Yet, in so doing you have given treasure to the stranger, and so robbed the nest; this may override all those things which I cannot help in my pride applauding, if not cheering, in you. . . . What do you say, dear wife and mother of my only son . . . ?

Too bad, she said.

Too bad what? cried father.

That a tree so young is dead, she said.

62297

For some reason there was a vein of teeth that had developed without jaw or appetite in the earth, like precious stones or metals.

The toothless came here to bite the earth and to come away with teeth stabbed into their gums.

No telling what one would come up with, tusks, tiny mouse teeth. . . . A toothless man no longer toothless cried through hippotamus teeth, I have got myself handsome with a smile full of hippotamus teeth!

Ah, but teeth are designed to a diet. He with cows' teeth ate grass saying, I do not like grass, but I eat grass because it fits my teeth. A cripple who must wear an ugly shoe; nevermind the glass slipper. If the shoe fits, wear it.

And so they wore their teeth like shoes. Many allowing this wisdom walked on their teeth. Others, moving one more step in logic, kicked their feet into the earth, driving teeth into their feet.

These are funny shoes, said some, but if the shoe fits . . .

Others began to chew their food by stamping on it.

And so they came one more step in logic, and stuffed shoes in their mouths, crying, we have got leather teeth.

It was terrible that dentistry had come so far only to die at the foot of human logic.

THE DIFFICULTY WITH A TREE

A woman was fighting a tree. The tree had come to rage at the woman's attack, breaking free from its earth it waddled at her with its great root feet.

Goddamn these sentiencies, roared the tree with birds shrieking in its branches.

Look out, you'll fall on me, you bastard, screamed the woman as she hit at the tree.

The tree whisked and whisked with its leafy branches.

The woman kicked and bit screaming, kill me kill me or I'll kill you!

Her husband seeing the commotion came running crying, what tree has lost patience?

The ax the ax, damnfool, the ax, she screamed.

Oh no, roared the tree dragging its long roots rhythmically limping like a sea lion towards her husband.

But oughtn't we to talk about this? cried her husband.

But oughtn't we to talk about this, mimicked his wife.

But what is this all about? he cried.

When you see me killing something you should reason that it will want to kill me back, she screamed.

But before her husband could decide what next action to perform the tree had killed both the wife and her husband.

Before the woman died she screamed, now do you see?

He said, what . . . ? And then he died.

DISTRACTION / for my Father

The family collapses like a house.

At first starlight is seen through father's head. The sky is beginning to bring its things through our roof.

It is raining in the hallway closet. The rain has come to visit the raincoat hanging there. The raincoat invites the rain, ceasing to recognize the boundary. . . . Why should it? — Our things learn what we pretend; see how the walls are turning to flesh, distracted by the sky, or from wherever it is that the distraction enters the attention. . . .

The rich hire orchestras, and have the musicians climb into trees to sit in the branches among the leaves, playing Happy Birthday to their dogs.

When the manservants come with birthday cakes, they are told, not now, do not dare disturb me when I am listening to my dog's music.

I was just wondering, sir, if I should light the candles?

I said not now. Do you want to distract me from my dog's music? Don't you realize that this is his birthday, and that it's been a whole year since his last birthday?

Shall I just put the cake in his feeding bowl, sir?

You are still distracting me from my dog's music. I wonder why you do it. This is not your birthday. Why are you trying to attract my attention?

But, sir, the cake . . .

But do you think I want my dog to see me talking to you while his music is being played? How would it seem to you if I talked to the dog while your music was being played?

So sorry, sir, I'll take the cake back to the house. . . .

Oh no, it's gone too far for that — Sic'em, sic'em, cry the rich to their dogs.

And so the dogs of the rich leap on the serving men, who cry, help help, to the rich, who reply, not now, not now, the dog's birthday is passing into history, with all its marvelous music!

ELEPHANTS

A herd of elephants stands in the yard, old pieces of tusk lying in the grass at their feet.

They endure through winter and summer, slowly evolving their monumentality.

It is said that the eye of a fly can actually see the hour hand moving.

The body collects itself gradually from carrots and chops; works late into the night, translating these things into fingernails and pubic hair.

The night is falling, and nature sucks its teeth at my window. I pretend to be living my own life.

They have lost their baby down a sewer. They might run to the sea where the sewer empties. Or they might wait where they have lost him; perhaps he returns out of the future, having found his manhood under the city.

Surely they risk his having turned to garbage, an orange peel with a bag of chicken guts.

She is not sure she could love an orange peel with a bag of chicken guts.

It's okay, honey, because everything happens under the smile of God.

But why, in heaven's name, is He smiling?

Because He knows the end.

But aren't we still getting there?

Yes; but He's seen it several times.

Seen what several times?

This movie, the one He produced and directed. The one He starred in. . . . You know, the one where He plays all the parts in a cast of billions . . . The story of a husband and wife losing their baby down a sewer . . .

Oh that movie; I cried through the whole thing.

THE FADING

The old man's hair is white, so is his face. One imagines if the process continues he shall become transparent.

He reminds one of a mist in a valley.

He is beginning to merge into his own memory, like a window crowded with ghosts.

His substance is failing. One wonders how he manages to be present at all.

We bought an electric monkey, experimenting rather recklessly with funds carefully gathered since grandfather's time for the purchase of a steam monkey.

We had either, by this time, the choice of an electric or gas monkey.

The steam monkey is no longer being made, said the monkey merchant.

But the family always planned on a steam monkey.

Well, said the monkey merchant, just as the wind-up monkey gave way to the steam monkey, the steam monkey has given way to the gas and electric monkeys.

Is that like the grandfather clock being replaced by the grandchild clock?

Sort of, said the monkey merchant.

So we bought the electric monkey, and plugged its umbilical cord into the wall.

The smoke coming out of its fur told us something was wrong.

We had electrocuted the family monkey.

THE FLOOR / for Charles Simic

The floor is something we must fight against. Whilst seemingly mere platform for the human stance, it is that place that men fall to.

I am not dizzy. I stand as a tower, a lighthouse; the pale ray of my sentiency flowing from my face.

But should I go dizzy I crash down into the floor; my face into the floor, my attention bleeding into the cracks of the floor.

Dear horizontal place, I do not wish to be a rug. Do not pull at the difficult head, this teetering bulb of dread and dream. . . .

FROM THIS SHORE

That lovely sailboat seen from this shore; that lovely sailboat using your eyes to be seen . . .

It does not see you, no more than a cow sees a baby drinking the milk of its udders in a distant city.

It is giving you itself, enjoying that self in the distance as two tiny sailboats no bigger than the pupils of your eyes.

Look how it does not allow the ocean to pull it down. The ocean puts everything in its mouth.

Everything we see we remember, filling our heads with miniature toys; a microscopic sculpture of sailboats, of oceans, of cows, of babies drinking milk in distant cities. . . . In your head a microscopic ocean laps a microscopic shore . . . There, a microscopic self watches a microscopic sailboat . . . And even in the head of that microscopic self a smaller description is forming, atoms tilting in mnemonic sculpture . . .

GRAVY

Ah, the gravy! — The liquid that arrives in a boat; a gravy boat run aground on the dining room table next to the meat — And here come the potatoes!

Is gravy always a liquid? Why not a cloud? A brown cloud of gaseous gravy floating through dining rooms filled with drought — Raining in landscapes of cooked meats and dry potatoes . . . Yes, like those white fellows in the window, who conduct their affairs from the earth; heads together, full of rain, they drift. . . .

If it is true then that gravy does come in clouds, as well as in boats, we will dance, even as the Indians danced for rain. . . . Often the appreciative rain fell in applause.

We will call our dance the Gravy Waltz. And we will sweep and glide in such brocades as ever tempted gravy to an arid meat.

A brown little cloud drifts out of the kitchen; comes over the meat, hovers there — A streak of lightning no bigger than a mouse's tail — A roll of thunder no louder than a well gassed fart — Drip drip drip falls the gravy on the arid meat.

A HARP'S PROGRESS,
OR THE LONG VIEW

The harp wonders if I will help it to the bathroom.

I'm not sure that I should be seen looking for a bathroom with a harp.

The harp feels faint and wonders if it wouldn't be beyond my sympathy to see it to the bathroom.

But I must wonder how it will seem to be seen with this large stringed instrument in the back halls of a theater. I must wonder if it will not seem altogether tragic as the night watchman says, but how ill your mother looks; or the cleaning woman who noticing this pale harp on my arm: but, what have you done to your wife?

No no, I say to the harp who continues harping at me. . . . After all, half the fun is getting there, getting there on your own!

The harp sighs. And then I sigh. And then time moves once more, creating from the given material whatever it is that time feels appropriate, in what can only be described as the long view.

There was a medicinal girl named Aspirin who, when the head was in its pain, was wound.

Left nipple hinging out into a little crank, through which Miss Aspirin's hips, hung with lead cheeks, are wound.

Left nipple hinges back into its breast, looking like a pink cigar-holder again.

Hip-starter between her cheeks. One goose and she dances — Swings her lead buttocks, smashes tables and chairs, knocks down the walls, levels the house, kills the man: headache cured.

. . . She stands in the wreckage with an inquiring smile, her buttocks sagging, her spring run down.

ILLUSION

Every so often he sees a bird fly up the chimney out of the ashes in his hearth.

He wedges a couple of iron pipes in the flue. When the birds fly up now they are trapped, fluttering at the pipes.

He has only to throw a few sticks of wood into the ashes and the flaming bird falls back and is cooked. It is endless.

The flesh is pure white and without any taste. The scraps seem to melt away without trace. The strange chalky bones if looked at long enough are transparent.

For awhile this seems a good supply of meat; but after eating 19 birds he is still hungry. He wonders if he hasn't been eating optical illusions. . . . He remembers the story of a man lost in a desert who finds a mirage, and because of his great thirst rushes recklessly into it and drowns. . . .

A husband and wife who are without child adopt a wheel.

Are we not like those of antiquity who took the wheel to service the burden, as we the burden of our need, so take this wheel? cried the husband.

Do you mean that antique parents could rise out of history to embrace back our child? cried the wife.

They dare not, though the burden of the earth grow heavy, screamed the husband.

Is the earth in league with our despair, growing heavy to remind an ancient claim? cried the wife.

No, love makes it right; for you comb its wooden spokes, and I spank its rim, ministering parental justice, cried the husband.

No no, a hand rises out of the earth, cried the wife.

No no, with scythe and hate I cut it down to the pleasure of the maternal fly, cried the husband.

But it repairs, being more than flesh; and it rises from the earth again, casting the shadow of its claim, cried the wife.

If it cannot be turned back, surely it will come, said the husband.

And if it comes and its claim is right . . . ? said the wife.

No no, I would rather put the child in the fireplace, screamed the husband.

Yes yes, Isidore! screamed the wife.

So husband and wife put a wheel into the fire and watch it burn.

KILLING THE APE

They were killing the ape with infinite care; not too much or it runs past dying and is born again.

Too little delivers a sick old man covered with fur.

. . . Gently gently out of hell, the ape climbing out of the ape.

THE KINGDOM

. . . That's funny, my watch is melting on my wrist.
I wonder if it's painful?
I have been living in my mind.

Out in the provinces of my extremities, where any event seems central, a simple folk of fingers, yolked in habits, are beginning to find evidence that nature is at last changing its mind.

Out in the province of my left wrist, my watch is melting — hands reaching out, curl back to their breast of numbers, in the sudden heat. An old man's supplication.

Time the bringer, finally ruins everything.

I have been living in my mind. Pain rides in. I no longer care; the king is sick with doubt.

49

A gravy boat had run aground, and now gravy was spilling through the landscape.

A treadmill making its way through the landscape saw a couple of onions floating on a dark gravy.

Hello sirs, said the treadmill.

The onions not used to speaking to strangers continued floating along with the gravy.

I say sirs, said the treadmill, there's been a bit of trouble in the landscape; it seems a steam organ stomped its master to death. . . . Oh well, thought the treadmill, I suppose the little sirs have better things to do than talk with strangers.

The gravy was lost. It thought it saw lights through the trees, but they were only stars.

The little onions cried, are we going to the stars?

Hush, said the gravy.

Now they heard music. The little onions cried, music and laughter.

Oh I could use a little laughter, said the gravy.

And so the gravy began to spill towards the music.

The little onions were crying, hurry, hurry.

As the treadmill was crossing a bridge out of the landscape it heard carnival music; and there below the bridge the ferocious steam organ was sucking the gravy up into its pipes. The little onions were screaming.

Ah, said the treadmill, I miss my little glockenspiel. And the treadmill continued over the bridge, the one that connects this landscape to the reader.

A LOVE LETTER

Dear Miss,

First of all I want to say that I have enjoyed the imaginary possibility, built of course on the fact that such possibility does exist in nature: I have seen the birds and other forms of nonhumanity occur in such postures that must be with men and women. . . . I have imagined myself in such postures with you, where flight was discouraged only by the inherent possibility of the firm horizontal. . . .

As men give vast lands to little papers with line and color, I have imagined more on the surface of your body, giving all the universe in this model. . . .

Yet, I must be curious about your breasts . . . curious . . . *hungry* is the word, to see, to touch, to taste. . . . I am curious as to how your hands undress your body.

I am interested in your mind: will you undress in front of me? Will you permit me the unparalleled pleasure of taking your clothes off?

I feel that if I should have my penis in your vagina I should have your love; for you do not receive the wretched hardness of my desire into the sweet body of yourself without that you have not come to love me for reasons, if love has reasons, I cannot tell. . . .

Your admirer

LOVERS

There was a blind owl which was loved by a squirrel with a crushed head.

If the squirrel thought the owl was a squirrel, the owl thought the squirrel was an owl — Did it matter? — I mean, in the night, would it matter when the squirrel was upon its mate; the owl on her back pressing closer the squirrel with wings dormant for love . . .

And could it matter after the act when the great woman owl murmured, don't move, stay . . .

The squirrel is restless.

The owl sighing, don't move, honey . . .

The squirrel wants a drink of water, I'll be back in a minute . . .

Stay with me, honey . . .

Many nights of this.

An infant feeds its mother from one of the dots on its chest.

Oh no, this will never do, laughs its mother, you'll starve me to death.

The infant slaps its mother.

I do not wish that, cries its mother.

But the infant slaps its mother again.

Very well, you win, I shall starve to death, cries its mother.

But the slapping mechanism in the infant has gotten stuck, so the infant slaps its mother again.

Look look, I'm feeding contentedly, even though I'm starving to death, cries its mother.

But the infant, owing to the sticking of its slapping mechanism, continues the slapping of its mother.

Stop stop stop, you are ruining what was otherwise a complacent and docile personality — You are causing me to be afraid, and when I grow up I shall be that old maid who sees in the male organ the aggression which you now administer, cried the mother.

The mind is mostly desert. The moon is lovely there, and almost turns the sands to water, save for one's natural logic.

At the paper-doll factory we are issued scissors, and warned not to monkey with our wrists.

I am an extremely serious person, needing no lectures on the care and maintenance of my tools.

I let the wrist business go unchallenged. Why should I invite discourse about monkeys with inferiors who, though in executive station, are nevertheless inferiors in the art of the scissors.

One's work involves the folding of paper, snipping here and there, and finally unfolding a self-portrait of insomniacs in a line of beds, each a night, arranged end to end.

Another ingenious design is a traffic of cars joined bumper to bumper, and so on, depending on how many folds one has made.

One dependable old woman with a rather unlovely stare, creates a masturbator pattern: a chain of lonely men holding their penises, ingeniously attached penis by penis; one long spit through all their groins.

There is the morning-bus motif, the public-toilet motif, any number of old favorites. . . . Yet, I thought to give the factory a motif closer to the popular taste; and by this means prove myself worthy of executive station. I created a suicide motif: a chain of paper-doll factory workers attached elbow to elbow, cutting their wrists.

An inferior foreman merely said, you are well on your way to the misuse of your tools, which may well involve your monkey.

. . . My monkey? I screamed.

. . . Of course the mind is a desert; one grows used to the simplicity of thirst.

. . . So the big monkey is sitting on the little monkey.

How far does it go?

As far as the need for sitting monkeys extends up and down the scale of size.

No sooner does an egg break, and a monkey emerges, than he is sitting on another monkey, as even another monkey is sitting on him.

As high and as deep as you look there is nothing but monkey fur.

Under the water a dead monkey looks up at us. Is this the end? Does this mark a departure, the development of an aquatic monkey, freed at last from the caste system?

We have never lived long enough to know the final outcome.

Oh bother the flies!

In the wheel is the round shape.

The road is calling only that it is open; and you flow naturally into it, closing something behind you as you fall from the foreground.

You fall from a door. You fall down a road.

You can get nothing, can hold nothing; your finger bones fall away like cigarette butts.

But, in the wheel forever, see it, the shape moving through its own shape like a stillness.

. . . Falling through your whole life, you are breaking apart . . .

But in the round shape of the wheel is the idea which is the bone upon which the flesh of the wheel is fixed . . .

MRS. GRUNDY

A hat is not to be dismissed by simply quitting it from the head and putting it on a hook.

A hat will knock you down. It will just get too annoyed with you.

A hat is not alone, it is family with pitchers and cups, with a distant blood tie to vaginas.

You will take your hat off and spend an hour talking softly to it. You will excuse yourself as you leave it. You will kiss it goodnight, goodnight my love.

Otherwise you will have to make very sure your hat is not a pair of bedroom slippers treading softly through the house at night.

MY UNCLE IN THE DISTANCE

My uncle had a mustache made of spinach. It was green and full of sand. It was lovely in the distance when one had lost sight of it among the leaves of trees.

But at close range, particularly at the dinner table, it seemed something caught on his upper lip, which he should have had the decency to lick off.

But my uncle doesn't like spinach, especially when it's so full of sand.

Poor uncle, finally in complement to his mustache, slowly gave up his animality. Soon it was no longer uncle, but a hodgepodge of squashes and root plants, leafy and fungal portions, waddling about the house.

Until father cried, my God, cut him up for supper!

After that the difficulty seemed to disappear into the distance of the years . . . lovelier and more distant each of the years that are the distance they create.

His left nostril was visiting in his right nostril. And he was feverishly swatting flies hoping that one of the flies was not a fly but the dark of his missing nostril.

At last despairing he drew a dark spot on the left wing of his nose with a pencil.

Suddenly his left nostril crawled out of his right nostril, and he saw that he had three nostrils.

He erased the extra one.

He heard a scream.

My God, my God, I've killed a nostril.

The dead nostril fell to the floor.

His other nostril crawled up into his nose. Even the pencil mark edged out onto his cheek pretending to be a beauty spot.

He called to the nostril hiding in his nose, oh please come out, it was all an accident.

He even called to the pencil mark, please do not be afraid, I will buy you an ice-cream cone. . . .

OATMEAL, OR THE DEATH OF RAMROD

A man wonders if the foolish head, which is where he wonders, were removed, might he then not be free to set a bowl of oatmeal on the pedestal of his neck?

He would be careful to be level-headed, not to spill the oatmeal of his wits . . . Known then to be straight of back; quite the ramrod, most dignified; indeed, a delight among the ladies who quite sense that obstinacy of spine.

But should a lady drop her handkerchief he must go down without tipping his head.

All of life is such a thing, going down without tipping your head . . .

Ramrod is dying. The martial moment is a bowl of oatmeal spilling from the pedestal of a thought, a drum roll beating a froth of white winged birds in haste to flight . . .

He wipes his brains up with the lady's handkerchief.

A piece of a man had broken off in a road. He picked it up and put it in his pocket.

As he stooped to pick up another piece he came apart at the waist.

His bottom half was still standing. He walked over on his elbows and grabbed the seat of his pants and said, legs go home.

But as they were going along his head fell off. His head yelled, legs stop.

And then one of his knees came apart. But meanwhile his heart had dropped out of his trunk.

As his head screamed, legs turn around, his tongue fell out.

Oh my God, he thought, I'll never get home.

An old man's hand was slowly but surely becoming a white spider with purple markings.

When he passed it through the air in gesture, spindrifts of web floated.

Sometimes at table his hand, dragging his arm, would crawl toward us. We would withdraw under logical but polite reasons.

One day we found him hanging by his arm from the ceiling. He seemed in an advanced state of desiccation . . . His hand above him in a fog of webs, fluttering, manipulating . . .

OUR NEIGHBORS

We are turning into several persons who died recently.

Our neighbors, always interested in comparisons, are climbing through our windows.

They steal our pens and eyeglasses. They steal iodine from the medicine cabinet. They need something.

The house is helpless, its people are dead.

A PICTURE POSTCARD

... Beasts of burden ... I sat where they drink and heard their tongues lapping the water that might have been the medium of Aristotle's urine, or even the saliva of the Tyrannosaurus rex.

How like workingmen they are, covered with the good sweat of muscular combustion, drinking their beer and snorting. They have earned their bodies all day, their eyes are quiet. They break their bread with certitude; they munch their hay; wives carrying food to the table; the farmer forking hay to his ox ...

I see them as I think God must, which may sin me to hell; a commoner who enters the castle, and from that view, the head of God, as it were, sees the labored hills patched in grape and barley ... To see the world as a picture postcard; picturesque ... No true labor or necessity; it is all an art, a bric-a-brac of cuckoo clocks and imported Madonnas in plaster ...

... And the water, used again and again, like a stage prop. This time the tears of the crocodile; next time part of the waters that took the Titanic. ...

Sitting outside of it one sees the great bully nightmare as Tyrannosaurus rex. ... *Wish you were here,* so the postcard reads ... But then you are *here* even if you are *there,* time and space meet in the human head, pasted together with neurons.

There goes the Dawn horse with its five toes, yawning for having to be up so early.

Wish you were here ... But then you aren't even *there,* not *here* or *there* ... Reality is only human. ...

I have entered the castle and no one is here, not even myself, whom I thought had come in. ... But still, the view: Aristotle peeing, the Titanic sinking in crocodile tears ...

Wish you were here, the bric-a-brac is something else. ...

This man dreams that a pig will escort each man into happiness.

The pig will come on its hind legs. We take hold of one of its front hooves, and find paradise, dancing, I should imagine, all the way.

Each man, one by one, awakened in the night; seen by his neighbors dancing down the street with a pig.

Is it inglorious to be seen with the pig of glory?

I say to the pig, pig, you are God's special evidence; you are not a hoax, are you, pig? No no, you couldn't be, your dancing is just too professional for that.

At last paradise which, oddly enough, is full of pigs. They are herding men to slaughter. First we pay for the bacon — Sure, why not, that makes sense. . . . Then happiness; all the pigs leave paradise . . .

. . . But then it's a chicken hell, where chickens pay us out for all the eggs we've eaten; they peck our mouths and fill their gizzards with our teeth. . . . But then it's even a hell of vegetables, where carrots and bananas gang against us, they want our testicles. . . . Hell of the inanimate, tables and chairs that require our eternal hopelessness. . . . This is how we go to paradise.

Oh pig — Never so happy, so happy as now, anticipating happiness — Dancing in hell with the paradise pig — Oh pig, dear pig, I am not worthy!

PINOCCHIO'S BRIDE

The little girl is given one of those marionettes, the kind that eventually attach their strings to people, the kind that make little girls into marionnete-wives of Pinocchio.

The marionette wears make-believe clothes over his imitation body; a shirt and tie dickey, a toy jacket with toy trousers.

The little girl undresses the marionette because she is not allowed to undress her parents.

She removes the marionette's trousers to check its backside for *duty*.

The marionette smiles cunningly as the little girl enmeshes herself in wickedness.

And now, the little nub of cotton-stuffed cloth at the marionette's crotch, swells and bursts, and a red stick, like a Pinocchio nose, points out.

THE PLEASURE OF OLD AGE

When you get old you come apart. Your elbows become frayed, and bones begin to show. Your knee caps are as bare of flesh (too much love), as your head, of hair (too much thought).

And as you are dressing one day one of the nipples comes off your chest, and drops to the floor like a shirt button. The old woman sews it back, remarking how like paper is the skin of your chest; she is sure the stitching will tear out.

You save your toes in a bottle, they are always breaking off in your shoes; they look like teeth.

One morning as you sit for your daily stool you are not surprised to see that you have delivered your purple liver into the toilet; and a broken tube from your lower bowel hangs from your anus.

When you get old your dry and cracked ribs stick out of your chest. You break them off like kindling.

The old woman is constantly coming to sew your lip or ear back on. She complains your skin just won't hold the thread.

She sews your penis and scrotum on, but the thread breaks through the flesh. It just won't come right, she says.

Still, you enjoy her fussing with your penis.

THE PREPARATION

When he bought a pair of shoes it was an undertaking to be prepared for by years of meditation.

But even so, he forgets and buys a hat.

In the end, when discipline has met senility, he is sold a pair of shoes: an infant's slipper and a toy sailboat . . .

THE PRESS OF NIGHT

At night when the strings are cut; the only string is an electric cord feeding an electric light.

. . . No, there is no other place.

The electric light presses on the window to keep out the night.

Memory is a string caught in some dark place, beyond even memory; a tangled kite string that will not let the kite rise, even as the metamorphic winds of life will not let it fall.

Thus falls the attention into itself; the lens of the attention withdrawing from the distance; lives in the foreground, having broken from extreme depth.

Chair and table become textures. The eyes grown tactile read the room as Braille. The attention flutters like a moth caught in a room; neither through the window nor into the head of the dreaded self . . .

All out there the night . . .

A rat owns a man, which it operates with apron strings from its rathole in the wall.

The rat has the man to sit on a chair and to have his hands on his knees, and to sit there and to think, which for the largeness of the man's head he is supposed to do.

When the man's mother visits him he says he is a rat's thing.

Because the woman would tie the man to her apron and cause him to go away with her, the rat pulls the excuse-me-string, and the man excuses himself for the bathroom.

Then the rat pulls the prepare-to-cut-string, and the man takes out his razor.

Then the rat pulls the cut-one's-throat-string, and the man cuts his own throat.

When the mother finally goes to see what keeps her son she finds him dead with his throat cut.

She sees apron strings coming out of one of his pant legs, and follows them back to a hole in the wall where a rat's eyes are beady, looking out at her.

She ties the strings to her apron and begins to dance. This drags the rat out by the fingers of its paws.

As she dances the rat is swung against the walls, until it is dead.

The blood of her son returns to his throat. His throat becomes uncut. He returns the razor to its place.

He says, I dreamed I was a rat's thing.

No, you are my thing, she says as she ties him to her apron.

STEPS

... From each bedroom a stairway coming through the downstairs ceiling. The first floor is a forest of steps. One stairway coming through the ceiling ends on the dining room table near some shallacked flowers. Another in the living room is stubbed into the cushions of the sofa. Stairways growing like roots, the kind that break rocks — Another stops on the mantel shelf; another grows into the library — One hanging like a caterpillar, forms a new step even as I watch. . . .

Proprietor proprietor, your house is odd!

Yes, he says, it always begins as a tiny crack in the ceiling . . . Something easily gotten used to, like the first wrinkle of your face; until at last the old man conquers your mirror.

But the steps!

... Then the smallest of nubs . . . no more than an upstairs fat person sitting too heavily, the leg of his chair coming through the ceiling . . . or is it the fat man's walking stick? . . . Perhaps it is a lonely man who falls forward on his penis. . . .

But the steps!

... Now the nub is widening . . . forms the lip of a step, like a smile. I smile back and ask the Angel of the ceiling if it is smiling at me. It buds and expands — An accordion of growing steps. I do not pretend to the reason for any of the things that have happened in the universe.

Proprietor, your bedrooms are likely filled with foetal steps!

The roots of the attic . . . My father trapped, a staircase on his chest; another growing through my mother's bed . . .

Why are you not chopping them away?

Too late, one of the stairways pins the ax to the floor.

71

A bed had just been removed from a woman's body by Doctor Boo.

The woman's mother said, there's a chair attached to my organ of sits and farts; can you remove it, Doctor Boo?

The woman's father said, there's a newspaper attached to my hands like big paper handcuffs, which I'm tired of reading; can you remove it, Doctor Boo?

Doctor Boo said, Doctor Boo must remove Doctor Boo from from this house.

Yes yes, Doctor Boo! — And may we watch the brave Doctor Boo performing on the brave Doctor Boo without an anesthetic?

A mother and son had a head factory, where spare heads were made for important people who had lost their's through diplomatic blunder, or in such mishaps that occur only at the finest hotels.

These heads were made of sawdust and paste, and were in great demand, as it had become fashionable for one to appear with a head not quite his own. The facsimile head was all the rage.

And it was not unusual for a man while shaving, as it were, to accidentally cut his head off. Or for a woman while slicing beef to slice through her own neck.

Yes, it seemed that decapitative accidents occurred quite frequently.

If mother and son slept late, as was their wont, headless mobs pressed at their door, complaining the shortage that allowed their necks to end so abruptly.

It irritated the mother and son that they should be roused from contemplative idleness to again bring their hands to the service of the vain decapitatee.

No, why should we spend our days making artificial heads when our own real heads wish only to nurse the breast of dreams.

THE TECHNICAL LIMITATION

Some ants having found a fallen sparrow enter the anus with a view to revamping this *aeroplane* to airline service between distances not yet fully understood.

. . . Now a cloud might serve as an excellent adjunct to a further adjunct . . . One need not now put together the whole of one's journey which, after all, grows like a flower towards its need.

Does poetry serve the shiny helmeted wits?

The highlight on your chitinous head keeps getting in my eyes. Then it's back to the ant hill . . . ?

Of course it's back to the ant hill. Did you think there was enough brain in an ant's head to make this aeroplane fly?

I thought that if I kept the highlight of my head out of your eyes you might have come to some technical understanding.

It's not so much the highlight as the head itself; there simply isn't enough brain tissue; a technical limitation that one just doesn't think one's way out of.

THE TURKEY HAPPENING

There were feathers growing on his wall. Thickly. And with pink turkey flesh beneath.

The feathers were spreading across the ceiling. And the floor was beginning to protrude in scaly bird toes like the roots of trees.

He could not tell if he had not now become himself feathers and turkey flesh.

He wondered if he was not now feathers and turkey flesh.

When you consider every leaf in that grove of trees, every insect there, eating and excreting, and all the birds likewising . . . And oh, those terrible clouds drifting closer and closer . . . All throwing their visibilities into my room . . .

Look how the walls belly out!

One doesn't mind one tree, a few blades of grass . . . or even that passing bird, throwing its visibility through the window . . . But, was it a bird, or was it an aeroplane full of visible people? It passes and I shall never know.

But look how the walls have bulged again.

It's never one tree; it's always groves and groves of redundant replication. Never a few blades of grass, but fields and fields of it. Not one bird, but flocks and flocks of them, jamming the sky with their trembling dark.

When you consider the very walls of my room, bulging with visions of the world; they are themselves visible, bulging, the more, at the sight of themselves.

Do I do less in a mirror, that shows a frightened man, as it spills those rays describing the organs of his visual sense; until the walls bulge, paradoxically, with the very organs of his sight; eyelashes scattered like cobwebs on the ceiling.

Look look, children playing among the trees!

Get away from there!

I'm holding my ears; one more cloud, and they'll carry me out in a basket.

VOMIT

The house grows sick in its dining room and begins to vomit.

Father cries, the dining room is vomiting.

No wonder, the way you eat, it's enough to make anybody sick, says his wife.

What shall we do? What shall we do? he cries.

Call the Vomit Doctor of course.

Yes, but all he does is vomit, sighs father.

If you were a vomit doctor you'd vomit too.

But isn't there enough vomit? sighs father.

There is never enough vomit.

Do I make everybody that sick, sighs father.

No no, everybody is born sick.

Born sick? cries father.

Of course, haven't you noticed how everybody eventually dies? she says.

Is the dining room dying . . . ?

. . . The way you eat, it's enough to make anyone sick, she screams.

So I do make everybody that sick. . . .

Excuse me, I think I'm going to be sick, she says.

Oh where is the Vomit Doctor? At least when he vomits one knows one has it from high authority, screamed father.

THE WAGON

I saw two nude people, a man and a woman.

I stopped my wagon, because it is mine, and I stop it when I wish . . . I have papers proving this.

I drew my wagon up and stopped, because as I said, my rights over the wagon not only include the right to make it move, but also to make it stop. No one must think that I am able to go on forever. Therefore, in the right to move is the understood right to stop.

As I was saying, I stopped my wagon to better view the nude people. I enjoy looking at nude people. Areas associated with sexual pleasure are of particular interest.

Of course I am only dealing with shadow and light; it is not as if I could put my hand on the woman's sexual hair. . . .

I have my wagon. It is mine to make move or stop. I can cause it to move a mile, and then I can stop it. And no one can say I must move it a mile and one foot. I can bring it to a halt exactly a mile from any designated point. Or, if I wish, cause it to move a mile and one foot from any designated point.

The penis of the woman's companion is interesting as it describes the woman in reverse image, and puts to the lie that women never say yes.

When it no longer serves my purpose to have my wagon stopped I make it move. I grant that if I make it move I shall cause it to stop again.

If the question should arise that asks why I should make it move only to stop it again; I must reply that in the exercise of my option I prove my right to the option. Besides, the nude couple have disappeared into the forest, and I would as soon be alone someplace else as here.

WHAT MOTHER MEANS

There is a woman who breaks silences—Yes she does!

My mother allows that this is likely not the entire periphery of what the woman must own to.

You mean, mama, the perimeter of her entire conduct must encompass more than direct blame accounts for?

I mean, said mother, the circumference of her activities must flesh more than silence breaking.

In other words, were the full profile known, silence breaking would seem the least of her moral impediments? I said.

I mean, said mother, should the full silhouette, the entire coastline, the total horizon, be known we should find in comparison, silence breaking more a blessing than a crime.

You mean the whole outline of her commitment? I said.

You know what I mean, mother screamed.

WHEN SCIENCE IS IN THE COUNTRY

When science is in the country a cow meows and the moon jumps from limb to limb through the trees like a silver ape.

The cow bow-wows to hear all voice of itself. The grass sinks back into the earth looking for its mother.

A farmer dreamed he harvested the universe, and had a barn full of stars, and a herd of clouds fenced in the pasture.

The farmer awoke to something screaming in the kitchen, which he identified as the farmerette.

Oh my my, cried the farmer, what is to become of what became?

It's a good piece of bread and a bad farmer man, she cried.

Oh the devil take the monotony of the field, he screamed.

Which grows your eating thing, she wailed.

Which is the hell with me too, he screamed.

And the farmerette? she screamed.

And the farmerette, he howled.

A scientist looked through his magnifying glass in the neighborhood.